GENTLE GIANTS
EDUTAINING FACTS ABOUT THE ELEPHANTS

Animal Book For Toddlers

Children's Elephant Books

BABY PROFESSOR
EDUCATION KIDS

Speedy Publishing LLC

40 E. Main St. #1156

Newark, DE 19711

www.speedypublishing.com

Copyright 2017

In this book, we're going to talk about elephants. So, let's get right to it!

Elephants are the largest land animals on our planet. There are two types of elephants. There are African elephants and Asian elephants. African elephants have ears that are shaped like Africa! Asian elephants have smaller ears than African elephants. Their ears are also rounder than an African elephant's ears.

Elephant

HOW BIG ARE ELEPHANTS?

It would be hard for an elephant to hide. An African elephant can be almost 25 feet long from its head to its tail. From its shoulders to its toes, it can be 13 feet tall. It's twice as tall as a man!

Asian elephants are just a little smaller. An Asian elephant can be 21 feet long from its head to its tail. From its shoulders to its toes, an Asian elephant can be 9 feet tall.

HOW MUCH DO ELEPHANTS WEIGH?

The African elephant weighs about 14,000 pounds. It weighs about the same as a school bus. The Asian elephant weighs about 11,500 pounds.

WHERE DO ELEPHANTS LIVE?

African elephants live south of the Sahara Desert in Africa. They live in rainforests in western and central Africa and the desert lands of Mali. Asian elephants live in Nepal as well as in India and the southeastern section of Asia. They live in rain forests and also in scrub forests.

Elephant in forest

Lin Wang

HOW LONG DO ELEPHANTS LIVE?

African elephants can live to be 70 years old. Asian elephants can live to be 60 years old. The oldest elephant that ever lived was an elephant named Lin Wang. He lived in a zoo in Taiwan until he was 86 years old.

DO ELEPHANTS HAVE NOSES?

Elephants have noses but they are trunks. The trunk is a blend of their noses and their upper lips. Their trunks have over 40,000 muscles. Elephants' trunks are like giant hoses and can get up to 7 feet long!

Elephant taking a bath

HOW DO ELEPHANTS USE THEIR TRUNKS?

Their trunks can do so many things. Their trunks can:

- Lift more than 700 pounds
- Suck 8 liters of water from a pond and squirt it into their mouths to drink
- Smell water several miles away

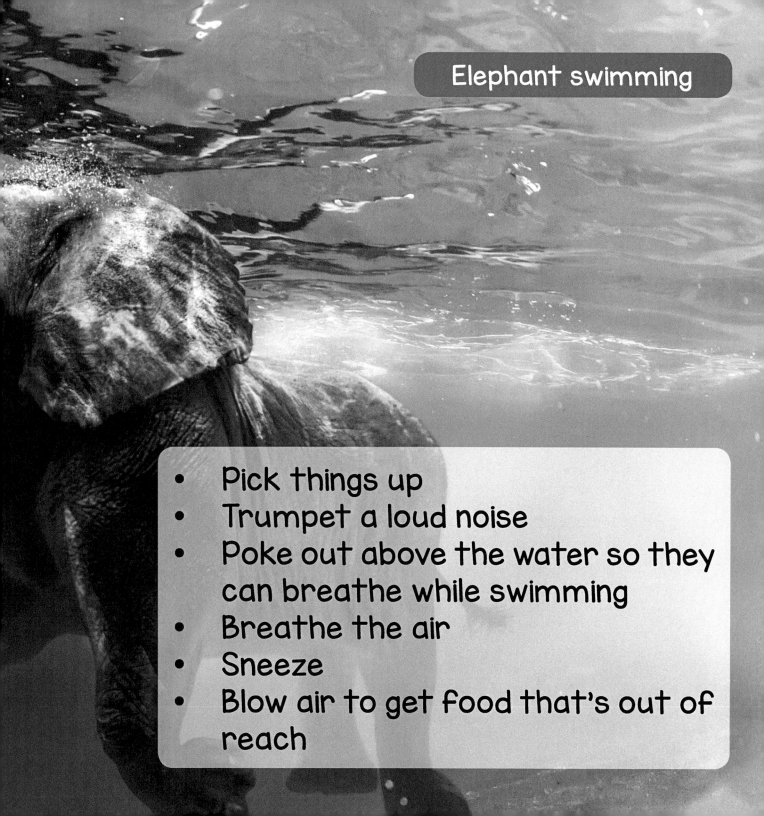

Elephant swimming

- Pick things up
- Trumpet a loud noise
- Poke out above the water so they can breathe while swimming
- Breathe the air
- Sneeze
- Blow air to get food that's out of reach

Elephant grabbing fruit

DO ELEPHANTS HAVE FINGERS?

Elephants don't have fingers like people. African elephants have two features like fingers on the ends of their trunks. They use these "fingers" to grab things. Asian elephants only have one finger on the end of their trunks.

HOW MANY TOES DOES AN ELEPHANT HAVE?

Elephants have five toes on each foot but you can't see them because their leathery skin covers them up. Some of the toes don't have toenails. They are actually standing on the tips of their toes with spongy pads at the bottom of their feet. Their legs are so straight that they can sleep standing up.

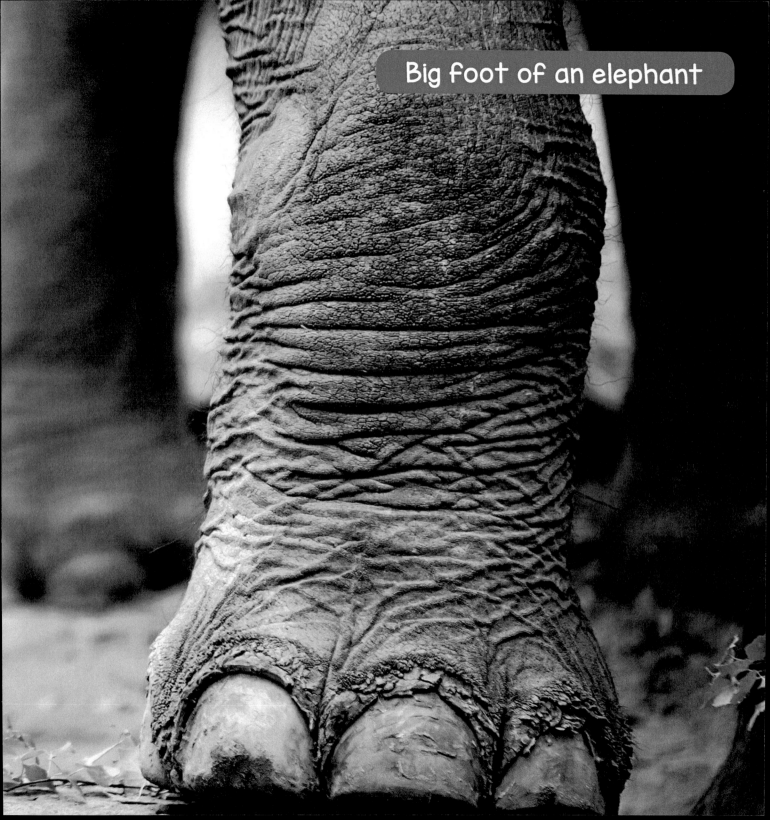

Big foot of an elephant

Elephant Family

DO THEY LIVE ALONE OR DO THEY HAVE A FAMILY?

Elephants have families. The oldest female elephant is in charge of the group. The family usually has a mother, the mother's sisters, their daughters, and their babies. Sometimes elephants that are not related join the family too. The family units have from three to as many as twenty-five elephants.

All the adults babysit the babies. The elephants learn what to do by watching the older female elephants. They walk in a single file and the baby elephants walk in the middle so they stay protected. The babies hold their mother's tails with their trunks so they can keep up.

Herd of elephants

Sometimes the herds of female elephants combine with groups of male elephants for protection. There can be as many as 1,000 elephants in a herd. Most of the time, male elephants travel by themselves or in groups with other male elephants.

HOW DOES THEIR SKIN FEEL?

Their skin is like leather and it is wrinkled. On some areas of their bodies the skin is very thick and in other places it is thin. Both types of elephants have grey skin. They wallow in the mud so the mud will protect their skin from burning. They sometimes look brown from the mud.

WHAT DO ELEPHANTS EAT?

Elephants eat up to 300 pounds of food every day! They eat grasses. They also eat the bark and roots of trees. They like fruit too. They are herbivores, which just means they eat plants. They don't eat any meat. Elephants drink up to 30 gallons of water every day.

HOW DO ELEPHANTS USE THEIR TAILS?

Elephants use their tails in lots of different ways. They have hair on their tails, so if flies are bothering them, they use their tails like a fly swatter. They also use their tails to communicate with other elephants. Babies sometimes hold on to their mother's tails.

Elephant's tail

Elephant's mouth

DO ELEPHANTS HAVE TEETH?

Elephants have two tusks, which are long, curved teeth that stick outside their mouths. They also have 24 teeth inside their mouths. The teeth inside their mouths are used for chewing. People only have baby teeth one time. Then their new adult teeth grow in. Elephants lose their teeth six times! New teeth grow in each time. Their teeth rotate in their mouths too. New teeth grow in the backs of their mouths and push out the old teeth.

WHICH ELEPHANTS HAVE TUSKS?

African elephants all have tusks. The male Asian elephants have tusks, but the females don't. Elephant tusks are made of ivory. People used to kill elephants to take their tusks because the ivory is valuable. Today it's against the law to kill an elephant to get its ivory. In fact, some elephants are born without tusks. Scientists think it's because they were hunted for so long.

Elephants playing

HOW DO ELEPHANTS USE THEIR TUSKS?

Elephants use their tusks for lots of different things. They use them to fight or defend themselves. They use them to dig and lift. They also use them to strip the bark off trees to eat. Sometimes if it's very dry out, they dig in riverbeds to find underground water. If they break a tusk and the root of the tusk is still there, it will grow back.

HOW FAST DO ELEPHANTS RUN?

Because elephants are so big, they don't run the way a horse runs. Their run looks like a very fast walk, but they can travel up to 15 miles per hour.

Elephant running

Elephant painting

WHERE CAN YOU SEE AN ELEPHANT?

You can see elephants at the zoo. If you get tickets, you can go to the circus to see an elephant do some tricks. Some people think that elephants shouldn't be kept in zoos or circuses because they are intelligent animals that have feelings.

CAN YOU HAVE AN ELEPHANT FOR A PET?

An elephant wouldn't make a good pet. Elephants like to be around other elephants. Unless you're an animal trainer or you're used to living around elephants it would be very hard to take care of an elephant. There are some places in the world where elephants do work like horses. They take people from place to place and carry large logs and other heavy loads.

WHAT TYPE OF ANIMAL IS AN ELEPHANT?

Elephants are warm-blooded mammals. They don't lay eggs. They give birth to babies. The babies drink milk from their mothers. Elephants are warm-blooded and they have hair. People are mammals too.

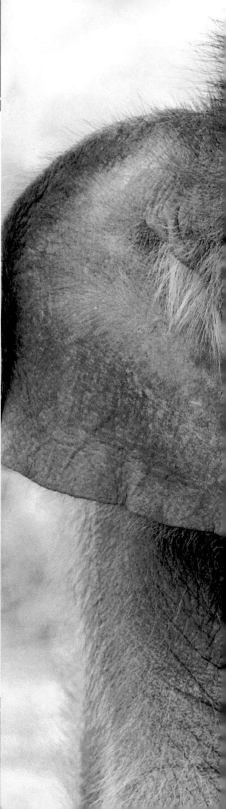

HOW BIG IS A BABY ELEPHANT WHEN IT'S BORN?

An elephant baby is called a calf. When it's born it weighs about 200 pounds and stands 3 feet tall.

Baby elephant

HOW DO ELEPHANTS STAY COOL?

Elephants flap their ears to keep cool. They suck up water through their trunks and spray it on their backs. They give themselves a shower! They can grab up dust to put it on their skin like baby powder.

HOW DO ELEPHANTS COMMUNICATE WITH EACH OTHER?

Elephants use their trunks, ears, tails, and body positions to send signals to other elephants. They also make lots of different sounds. Some are just gentle sounds to say hello. Some sounds are loud trumpets that travel over long distances to warn other elephants of danger. They also make sounds that humans can't hear.

DO ELEPHANTS HAVE FEELINGS?

Elephants have strong friendships with other elephants. Some elephants even have friendships that last their whole lives. If a mother elephant loses her baby, she's very sad. Sometimes elephants go back to where other elephants have died because they are sad.

ARE ELEPHANTS INTELLIGENT?

Scientists are still studying elephant intelligence. Elephants can solve problems either on their own or as a team with other elephants. They can also figure out ways to use tools. Elephants remember their friends, even if they don't see them for a long time. If an elephant is upset, the other elephants help. Elephants have good memories and scientists think they are almost as intelligent as chimpanzees and monkeys.

Awesome! Now you know more about elephants. You can find more Elephant books from Baby Professor by searching the website of your favorite book retailer.

Made in the USA
San Bernardino, CA
16 November 2018